MW01100437

WORLD IN VIEW

IRELAND

Mary Peplow & Debra Shipley

STECK-VAUGHN
L I B R A R Y
Austin, Texas

Published in the United States in 1991 by Steck-Vaughn Co.,
Austin, Texas, a subsidiary of National Education Corporation.

© Macmillan Publishers Limited 1989

First published 1989 by
Macmillan Children's books
A division of MACMILLAN PUBLISHERS LTD

Designed by Julian Holland Publishing Ltd
Picture research by Jennifer Johnson

Cover: *Rural scene in southwestern Ireland.*
Title page: *Horse and cart used to carry milk in southern Ireland.*

Library of Congress Cataloging-in-Publication Data

Shipley, Debra.
    Ireland / Debra Shipley, Mary Peplow.
        p.   cm.—(World in view)
    Summary: An overview of the geography, history,
economy, resources, culture, day-to-day life and people of the
country known as "The Emerald Isle."
    ISBN 0-8114-2430-8
    1. Ireland—Juvenile literature.   2. Northern Ireland—
Juvenile literature. [1. Ireland.]   I. Peplow, Mary.   II. Title.
III. Series.
DA906.S53   1990
941.5—dc20   90-32821
                                                        CIP
                                                        AC

Printed and bound in the United States
    2   3   4   5   6   7   8   9   0   LB   95   94   93

Contents

IRELAND

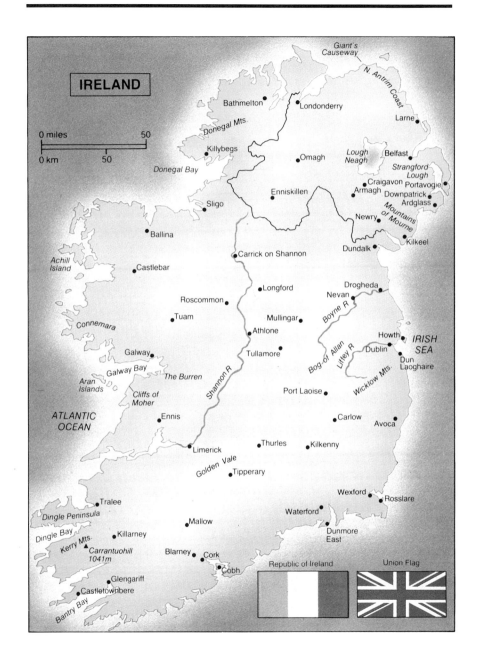

IRELAND

0 miles 50
0 km 50

Giant's Causeway
N. Antrim Coast
Bathmelton
Londonderry
Larne
Donegal Mts.
Killybegs
Lough Neagh
Belfast
Omagh
Strangford Lough
Donegal Bay
Craigavon
Portavogie
Enniskillen
Armagh
Downpatrick
Ardglass
Sligo
Mountains of Mourne
Newry
Ballina
Kilkeel
Dundalk
Achill Island
Carrick on Shannon
Castlebar
Longford
Drogheda
Nevan
Roscommon
Boyne R
Tuam
Mullingar
Connemara
Athlone
Howth
Galway
Tullamore
Dublin
IRISH SEA
Galway Bay
Bog of Allan
Liffey R
Dun Laoghaire
Aran Islands
The Burren
Wicklow Mts.
Cliffs of Moher
Shannon R
Port Laoise
ATLANTIC OCEAN
Ennis
Carlow
Avoca
Limerick
Thurles
Kilkenny
Golden Vale
Tipperary
Wexford
Tralee
Rosslare
Dingle Peninsula
Mallow
Waterford
Dingle Bay
Killarney
Dunmore East
Kerry Mts.
Carrantuohill 1041m
Blarney
Cork
Glengariff
Cobh
Republic of Ireland
Union Flag
Castletownbere
Bantry Bay

1   Introducing Ireland

Ireland is an island to the northwest of the mainland of Europe. It lies on the European continental shelf, which is a continuation of the land area beneath the water before it drops into the ocean basin. This means that the seas surrounding Ireland are generally less than 600 feet deep. Ireland's west coast is washed by the powerful waves of the Atlantic Ocean, and to the east the Irish Sea separates it from another, bigger island, Great Britain.

The warm waters of the Gulf Stream, an ocean current that starts far away in the Gulf of Mexico, and warm southwesterly winds help make Ireland's climate moderate. Also, as it is a fairly small island, there is very little difference between the weather in the north and in the south. Ireland is popularly known as "The

---

The national flag of the Republic of Ireland is made up of three colors: green, white, and orange. The green represents the Anglo-Norman people and the Gallic people (descendants of the early Celts) living in Ireland. The orange is for the descendants of the Protestant "planters" who supported William of Orange. The white stripe in the middle shows a lasting truce between the "Orange" and "Green."

The flag of Northern Ireland is the Union flag of Great Britain. This is made up of the crosses of St. George of England, St. Andrew of Scotland, and St. Patrick of Ireland.

The unit of currency in the Republic of Ireland is the Irish pound or *un punt Éireannach*. In 1979 the Irish pound ceased to be directly related to the British pound under the rules of the European Monetary System.

Emerald Isle" because it has a high rainfall that ensures plenty of green pasture. The driest area is the east coast near Dublin where the average annual rainfall is 30 inches. The more mountainous districts over on the west coast regularly receive more than 79 inches of rain each year. Nevertheless, the most outstanding characteristic of the Irish weather is its changeability. Misty early mornings can open up to become fine and clear days, or just as readily become dark and brooding by noon, only to change again by sunset.

Europe in miniature
The center of Ireland consists of a limestone plain with many low hills. The plain is partly surrounded by coastal mountains ranging from granite formations in the west and northwest to old red sandstone in the south. Indeed, Ireland has such a large variety of landscape, that it is sometimes called "Europe in miniature" because many of Europe's main geographical features can be seen in the compact space of this one island. There are fertile pastures, rugged cliffs, gentle lakes, fast rivers, high mountains, and coral beaches. There are also many bogs. The wet, often spongy, peat bog has long been useful in

7

The Burren is a large rocky area of land in County Clare. It was formed by earth movements millions of years ago. Today, it seems a harsh windswept place where few living things can be seen. When rain falls it drains away through the limestone rock and forms great underground caves.

Ireland, because the peat burns well and is used as fuel after it has been cut into brick-shaped pieces and dried.

Millions of years ago

There is one geographical feature in Ireland that is found nowhere else in Europe. The massive limestone formation in the west known as the Burren came into existence over 260 million years ago when a mass of rock was thrust up above the water level. The word Burren comes from an Irish word *boireann* which means a rocky place. It is an apt name, because the Burren is a strange rocky area that covers over 200 square miles. Another fascinating feature is the Giant's Causeway in the north, which looks like thousands of enormous pencils in bundles standing on end. In fact, the thousands of columns of rock were formed by cooling lava about 60 million years ago.

Most of Ireland was once covered by a large ice sheet which finally disappeared about 12,000 years ago. When the glacier melted, it left behind

Millions of years ago cooling lava contracted into these strangely symmetrical shapes. Roughly 40,000 hexagonal columns of volcanic rock are packed tightly together to form the Giant's Causeway. Many legends surround the causeway, and some say it was a roadway made by a giant known as Finn McCool.

deposits such as the many small hills known as drumlins which dot the lowland region. In the south there are gravel deposits also left behind by the melting ice. Ireland was once part of the European mainland but during the last Ice Age which ended about 10,000 years ago it became separated from Great Britain, which itself later became separated from Europe.

Fact Box

Republic of Ireland	27,136 sq miles
Northern Ireland	5,462 sq miles
Greatest length (north to south)	302 miles
Greatest width (east to west)	171 miles
Total coastline	3,500 miles
Distance between **Britain and** **Ireland**	13–120 miles

The nearest land to the west coast is North America 2,000 miles away.
Seasons: Spring, March–May; Summer, June–August; Autumn, September–November; Winter, December–February.

Wildlife and plant life

Possibly as a result of its separation from Europe during the Ice Age, Ireland has fewer types of animals and plants than other European countries. For example, it has only one reptile, a small lizard. In the rivers and numerous lakes there are many fish including salmon, char, pike, polan, and perch, while along the coast seals breed freely. Even whales can sometimes be spotted. Land animals include ermine, foxes, and red deer which are not protected. As many as 380 species of wild birds have been recorded in Ireland. Of these, although 135 breed in the country, the rest are migrating birds, because Ireland is a major stopping-off place for them. For instance, three-quarters of all the Greenland white-fronted geese in the world spend the winter in Ireland. Plover, ducks, meadow pipits, and skylarks arrive from the north during the autumn and winter months, while birds from the south, including chaffinches and starlings, come in during spring and summer.

Plants in Ireland vary according to what the soil is like. The bog lands seem at first sight to have very little vegetation but in fact bog moss, heather, and marsh plants all grow well there. Two areas of botanical interest are Glengarriff where many semitropical plants grow, and Killarney, whose woods are famous for the wild arbutus (of the heather family) that grows there. In the Burren region some arctic-alpine plants still survive from the last Ice Age, and there are also some species more usually found around the Mediterranean Sea. Ireland is one of the least forested parts of Europe, because there was extensive clearing of the natural forests in the seventeenth century. Replanting programs are in progress, however, and about 5.5 percent of the total land area is now forest. Throughout Ireland certain areas have been declared to be of outstanding natural beauty, like the Mountains of Mourne and the North Antrim Coast, and a number of national parks have been created, like that of Connemara. Connemara National Park covers about 5,000 acres of mountain, bog, heath, and grassland. It has a visitors center that is used by both serious mountain walkers and tourists. The park is also concerned with conservation, and tries to preserve the area's wildlife and plants as well as providing nature trails for visitors.

Ireland is a place of great natural beauty, and even in areas that have been farmed the fields have a special charm. Here, because the farmer has used no chemical fertilizers, thousands of wild poppies give a bright splash of color to the landscape.

Town and country

Ireland is divided into 32 counties. Since 1921, it has been divided politically into two parts. Twenty-six counties form the Republic of Ireland (*Saorstát Éireann*) while the other six counties are part of the United Kingdom of Britain. The latter are known in Britain as Northern Ireland and in the Republic as "the six counties."

The capital city of the Republic is Dublin. It is a

Young people in Dublin are fashion conscious and Grafton Street is their favorite place to shop and meet friends. No cars are allowed along it, so it makes an ideal site for street entertainment. Every Saturday a variety of entertainers can be seen performing.

very lively city particularly around its main street, O'Connell Street, and fashionable Grafton Street which has many thriving boutiques. Dublin is renowned for its Georgian architecture which has survived in good condition since the eighteenth century, especially in the richer parts of the city. However, not everyone in Dublin is rich, and beggars can often be seen, particularly women with children. Other important centers in the Republic include Cork, Limerick, Waterford, Dundalk, and Galway.

The major center of population in Northern Ireland is its industrial capital, the city of Belfast. Despite political troubles, Belfast has some attractive sections such as the area around the university and the Botanic Gardens. Two major

13

Ireland's troubled history has meant that many families have left their homes over the years. Many people have emigrated to the United States and Europe. The land is dotted with ruined houses, large and small. This rather grand ruin, Leamaneh Castle, is situated just outside Kilfenora.

museums in the city are the Ulster Museum and Art Gallery and the Ulster Folk and Transport Museum. Other major towns in Northern Ireland include Craigavon, Newry, Armagh, and Enniskillen. Both the Republic of Ireland and Northern Ireland belong to the European Economic Community (EEC).

The countryside of Ireland is sparsely populated, because large numbers of people left the rural districts during the nineteenth century either to go to the towns or to emigrate to America, Europe or Australia. Empty, decaying houses, both large and small, can be seen everywhere. Most country people live in cottages usually with some land attached on which they grow vegetables such as potatoes, carrots, and parsnips for the family to eat. Shopping can be quite difficult for country people as shops are to be found only in the towns. Most shops are small and their selection of goods may be limited. Quite often, in rural areas, the local pub will also act as a shop, selling basic groceries and provisions.

2   The Story of Ireland

Ireland has a wealth of prehistoric monuments. Newgrange in the Boyne Valley is over 4,000 years old. It is a passage grave that could hold thousands of cremated bodies. The tomb is so perfectly built that the interior is in complete darkness except one day of the year, the Winter Solstice on December 21.

Ireland was first inhabited around 6,000 B.C. by a group of people who traveled from Britain across the rough Irish Sea. They were hunters, catching fish and wild animals, and gathering berries from the land for food. These first settlers were afraid of the dark forests and bogs in the center of Ireland and made their homes near the coast. Then about 3,500 B.C., groups of Neolithic people (that is, people from the last period of the Stone Age) began to arrive from the regions around the Mediterranean Sea. They were farmers who cleared parts of the forests to grow crops and raise livestock.

Early civilizations

The Neolithic people were very religious. They placed great importance on burial rites and built large stone tombs for their dead. The simplest of these "great stone," or megalithic, tombs was the dolmen, many of which are still standing in Ireland. Dolmens were constructed by putting one heavy stone slab, known as the capstone, on top of three or four upright stones. Then there were magnificent burial chambers such as that at Newgrange in the Boyne Valley which could hold thousands of cremated bodies. Exactly how any of these tombs were built is still a mystery but they obviously required great engineering skill.

The next group of people to arrive in Ireland were known as the Beaker people. They were metalworkers and made beautiful ornaments and tools from bronze and gold. These early dwellers lived on *crannogs*, small islands that they built in lakes, rivers, and marshes. Some of these crannogs have been excavated and the remnants of a very early primitive civilization discovered.

Celts and the coming of Christianity

Of all the early invaders, it was the Celts, who came from northern Europe that had the most lasting influence. When they first invaded in the sixth century B.C., their iron weapons gave them a great advantage. The Celts continued to arrive for several centuries, bringing with them their culture and way of life. The country was divided into about 150 tiny kingdoms, each known as a *tuath* and ruled over by a minor king. In turn, these small kingdoms were grouped into five provinces, each again governed by a king. The

The Book of Kells is a beautiful illuminated manuscript that tells the story of the life of Christ. The detailed illustrations were the work of a group of talented Irish monks in the early Middle Ages. The colors are still vivid after hundreds of years.

five provinces were Ulster in the north, Leinster in the center and east, South Leinster in the southeast, Munster in the southwest, and Connacht in the west. The High-King or *Ard-Ri* had his seat at Tara in the County Meath. There were constant battles between the kings for supremacy. Although the Roman empire was widening its boundaries at this time, the Romans did not try to invade Ireland, and so the Celts were free to fight among themselves.

Ireland was converted to Christianity by St.

Patrick in the fifth century A.D. This was the start of an age of art and religious learning, and Ireland became known as the "island of saints and scholars." Many monasteries were founded and some of the monks became scribes and artists, producing beautiful illuminated manuscripts on fine parchment called vellum. *The Book of Kells*, written in the eighth century, is famous throughout the world. It is now in the library of Trinity College in Dublin. The monks learned other skills as well. They worked with metal to make elaborate chalices and jewelry, and began carving stone crosses. Over the years the carvings became more and more decorative. Irish monks also traveled to Great Britain and Europe as missionaries to spread their faith and learning.

Viking raids

Peace came to an end in the eighth century when Vikings from Scandinavia arrived in their longships on the east coast of Ireland. For two centuries they raided the monasteries, burning books and stealing treasures. The monasteries were also attacked by the Irish themselves. Round towers, for which Ireland is famous, were built at this time partly as protection from Viking and other attacks. These tall towers were used as bell towers, watchtowers, and also as hideaways for valuables and even people, although it must have been very cramped and uncomfortable. The Vikings set up fortified settlements and began to trade with nearby countries. One such settlement, at the mouth of the Liffey River, later grew into the city of Dublin.

The Vikings were eventually defeated by the

In Ireland there are about 70 round towers like this 97-foot tower at Ardmore. These tall, slim towers were built in the ninth to twelfth centuries as bell towers and as places for monks to hide both themselves and their valuables. The entrance was through a door some 13 feet from the ground and reached by a ladder that could be pulled up after the last person had entered.

High King, Brian Boru. Many stories have been written about this powerful king who won a crushing victory over the Vikings at the battle of Clontarf in 1014. Immediately after the battle, however, he was murdered in his tent. The other kings fought for the title of High King but no strong leader emerged and Ireland was very unsettled for several years.

This made it easy for the Anglo-Normans to take over large areas of land when they invaded in 1169. These new invaders were Normans from France who had been living in England since the Norman Conquest in 1016. One of the strongest was the Earl of Pembroke, known as "Strongbow," who became king of Leinster. The Anglo-Normans secured their position by building castles and walled towns, and in 1171 their overlord, Henry II, king of England, was recognized as overlord of Ireland. They dominated the east, center and south of Ireland and brought with them the parliament, law, and system of administration from England. The Irish made several attempts to overthrow the power of the Anglo-Normans and over the years gradually weakened their hold. Many Anglo-Normans married into Irish families and began to think of themselves as Irish.

The planters
When the Tudor monarchs came to the English throne, they tried to reestablish the strength of the English in Ireland. It was not, however, until the army of Queen Elizabeth I won a decisive victory at the battle of Kinsale in 1601 that a new era of English rule in Ireland began. To ensure lasting power, the Tudors took land from the Irish and gave it to settlers from England and the Scottish lowlands to form "plantations" of people, or colonies. From this, the new settlers became known as "planters." They were all of the Protestant faith because the English rulers were

determined to impose the Protestant religion on the Catholic Irish. The Protestant Church was proclaimed the official church in Ireland but most people still remained loyal to the Roman Catholic Church. Ulster was an exception. There the "planters" were mostly Presbyterians originally from Scotland who had already succeeded in living peacefully alongside the Roman Catholic community.

The Great Rebellion
The period from 1641 to 1652 is known as The Great Rebellion. Catholics in Ireland wanted a Catholic country and were prepared to fight for it. Thousands of Protestant settlers were murdered. The Protestants fought back and many more people were killed.

When the Protestant Oliver Cromwell came to power in Great Britain in 1649, he brought his "New Model" army to Ireland. He was determined to crush the rebellion and led brutal massacres in the towns of Drogheda and Wexford, slaughtering great numbers of people. Other towns were so terrified they surrendered. Catholics were forbidden to practice their religion, and a number of them lost their land. Others left the country. When the Catholic King James II became king of Britain it looked like things might become better for Catholics in Ireland. Most British people, however, did not want a Catholic ruler, and they asked William of Orange, James's son-in-law, to take the throne. James fled to France, where he raised an army and invaded Ireland in an attempt to regain power. William of Orange defeated him at the Battle of the Boyne in 1690, and James left the country.

The Catholics in Ireland were seen as a great threat and in the eighteenth century the British government enforced a series of laws that took away their civil and religious rights. They were not allowed to vote, to hold public office, or to run for a seat in parliament, and this also applied to Presbyterians and others who refused to belong to the main Protestant church. Catholic schools were closed down and churches and priests were banned. Many houses had concealed rooms known as "priest holes" in which to hide priests. By this time most Catholics were living in the rural areas in great poverty.

Grattan's parliament

The American War of Independence brought some changes to Ireland, not least because government troops had to be withdrawn to fight in America. Inspired by the Americans' example, the leading Irish Protestants decided that they, too, wanted more independence and authority in their own parliament in Dublin. They were at last granted this by Britain in 1782. One of the main figures in this more powerful parliament was Henry Grattan, who tried to have some of the laws against Catholics abolished. Dublin itself was enjoying great prosperity at this time and many beautiful buildings and squares were built.

Another world event that affected Ireland was the French Revolution. The ideas of equality and liberty for all appealed to a group of Irish people, who formed a number of societies calling themselves United Irishmen. Their object was to unite Catholics and Protestants, including

Presbyterians, so that they could break the link with England. The United Irishmen, led by Theobald Wolfe Tone, staged a rebellion in 1798 but they were too poorly organized to succeed. Their actions, however, worried the English government, which passed an Act in 1800 uniting the British and Irish parliaments and making Great Britain and Ireland into the United Kingdom.

The new act meant that Irish Members of Parliament (MPs) sat in the Westminster parliament in London, and Ireland no longer had a parliament of its own. In 1823, Daniel O'Connell, who later became the first Irish Member of Parliament, started a movement using nonviolent methods to reestablish the rights of Irish Catholics. Six years later the Catholic Emancipation Act was passed, which removed almost all the restrictions on Catholics.

Fleeing from famine
During the nineteenth century, life became more and more difficult for the Irish peasants. Most of them lived on tiny farms owned by absentee landlords who spent most of their time in England. The tenants had to pay excessive rents and were treated very badly. They had little control over their land or their homes. Starving families were turned out of their homes, cottages could be torn down, and the land could be given away to someone else. In addition to these problems, the peasants could barely produce enough food to feed themselves. Potatoes, which could be grown easily even on poor land, were the staple diet.

At one time, peasant farmers in Ireland lived mainly on potatoes. The soil in their fields was so poor this was the only crop they could grow. Then, from 1846 to 1848, the crop was hit by disease and many families had no food to eat. They couldn't afford to pay rent and were often forced out of their homes by their landlords.

Tragedy struck in 1846, when disease affected the crop so badly that the potatoes rotted in the ground before they could be eaten. Bad weather conditions made things worse and the potato crop failed again for the next few years. Many people either starved to death or died from disease. Thousands more left Ireland for good, sailing for North America and Britain to find a living. In 1845, Ireland had been overpopulated, with a population of about eight million people. By 1900, the population had fallen to half that number.

Home rule in Ireland

In 1858, Catholics who had fled to America formed a secret society called the Fenians. They intended to free Ireland from English rule by any means possible, even violent action. A similar movement was formed in Ireland called the Irish Republican Brotherhood (IRB). Not everyone in Ireland believed in using violence to change the situation, however. Many people wanted a semi-independent parliament based in Dublin; this was called Home Rule. In his attempt to gain this, an Irish MP, Charles Stewart Parnell, used various tactics of persistent obstruction, bringing parliamentary business to a halt.

Another man who did not believe in violence was Michael Davitt. He formed the Irish Land League whose aim was a fairer deal for tenant farmers. Parnell also supported this League. A number of Land Acts were eventually passed abolishing the old landlord system and giving the land back to the people.

Parnell died in 1891 without achieving Home Rule in Ireland. A Home Rule Act was eventually passed in 1912, but the outbreak of World War I in 1914 meant the law was suspended and it did not come into effect. Ireland was divided, with some people favoring Home Rule and others who wanted an Irish parliament that was completely independent from Britain. A new party was formed known as *Sinn Fein* which is Irish for "we ourselves."

In Ulster, in the north of the country, there were a large number of people who did not want either Home Rule or an Irish parliament. They felt they were British people and wanted to stay united with Great Britain. They did not want to be part of a separate Ireland. A number of private armies were formed in Ireland. Each was determined to fight for its own particular cause if necessary.

The Easter Rising

During the Easter Rising of 1916, rebel troops took over many mills and factories in Dublin, but they were eventually forced to surrender. The leader of these rebel troops was Eamon De Valera. He became President of Ireland but at the time of the rebellion he was a mathematics teacher.

During Easter week in 1916, the Irish Republican Brotherhood planned an armed rebellion. With Patrick Pearse and other republican leaders at their head, the group took over the main buildings in Dublin. They proclaimed a new Irish Republic and flew the new flag from the General Post Office. They fought government troops and police for five days but finally had to surrender. The British administration executed the leaders and deported or jailed hundreds of their followers. The rebellion aroused sympathy for the republican cause among the Irish people and at the General Election of 1918, the Sinn Féin

Eamon De Valera (1882–1975) was born in New York and came to Ireland as a young boy to live with his uncle in County Limerick. His old school is now a museum. De Valera became head of the Irish government in 1932 and President of Ireland in 1959.

party won by a large majority. The new members set up their own parliament, of *Dáil Éireann*, with Eamon De Valera as their leader.

At the same time, the Irish Republican Army (IRA) was formed. Its members used ambushes and attacked barracks in their fight against the British security forces. The government fought back fiercely, and Ireland found itself in a state of civil war.

Anglo-Irish Treaty

After several years of such fighting, the Anglo-Irish Treaty was signed in 1921. This divided Ireland in two. The new Irish Free State was made up of 26 of the 32 counties of Ireland, and it had its own parliament, although it was still called a dominion, that is, a member of the British Empire or Commonwealth. The remaining six counties of Antrim, Armagh, Down, Fermanagh, Londonderry, and Tyrone, became known as Northern Ireland and were part of the United Kingdom. They too had their own parliament, at Stormont in Belfast.

The Anglo-Irish Treaty meant that Ireland was again split by bitter civil war between those who supported it and those who wanted the whole of Ireland to be a completely independent republic. Hundreds of people were killed and thousands injured before the republicans were persuaded by De Valera to finally lay down their arms in 1923. The two main political parties of today's Irish Republic, *Fine Gael* (Tribe of Ireland) and *Fianna Fáil* (Soldiers of Destiny), are the same two parties that were originally for and against the Anglo-Irish Treaty.

27

The Republic of Ireland

The Irish Free State survived and became a member of the League of Nations. A new constitution was adopted in 1937 and the Free State became known as Éire, the Irish name for Ireland. The Irish parliament, which sits at Leinster House in Dublin, is made up of the President of Ireland and two houses of parliament: a house of Representatives and a Senate. The President is elected by the people for a seven-year office, and as Head of State appoints the prime minister. Everyone in the country over 18 years old can vote.

In 1949, Éire withdrew from the British Commonwealth and became the Republic of Ireland, a completely independent republic with its own government and laws. The Republic became a member of the United Nations in 1955, and in 1973 joined the European Economic Community.

3

Ireland Today and Tomorrow

These ''orangemen'' are in one of the many parades held in Northern Ireland to demonstrate political loyalties. They are wearing the traditional dress of bowler hats and orange sashes, and carry umbrellas.

Ireland has a history of conflict, and the situation in Northern Ireland today has its roots far back in the past. However, the basic problem lies in the partition of Ireland into Northern Ireland and the Republic of Ireland. Unionists in Northern Ireland are generally happy about the division and would like to stay part of the United Kingdom. Nationalists believe that the six counties of Northern Ireland should be part of one united Ireland of 32 counties.

The split between Nationalists and Unionists is

also one of religion and identity. Unionists are mainly Protestant and consider themselves to have more in common with British people than with the Irish. The fear that a united Ireland would bring with it what they feel is a foreign culture, as well as the influence of the Catholic Church and its teachings. Nationalists are generally Catholics who feel that they belong to the rest of Ireland rather than Great Britain.

Two communities

Although Ireland is going through troubled times, and newspapers all over the world are full of stories of the bitter fighting and tragic deaths, this is not the whole picture of life in Ireland. The

Parades

On certain days of the year Protestants and Catholics in Northern Ireland show their loyalties by marching in colorful parades. There are around 2,000 parades large and small throughout the year but the two most important dates are July 12 and August 15. The first is known as "Orangeman's Day." Orangemen are members of the Orange Order, a Protestant society loyal to the British crown. On July 12 each year they celebrate the victory of William of Orange at the Battle of the Boyne in 1690. They wear bowler hats, orange sashes, and white gloves, and carry umbrellas. Lady's Day on August 15 is named after the Virgin Mary, and members of the Ancient Order of Hibernians march in her honor. They wear green sashes to show allegiance to Catholic Ireland. Many marches are peaceful but sometimes emotions run high, leading to violence.

The official symbol on the coat of arms of the Republic of Ireland is a harp, as the country was famous for its minstrels. The coat of arms of Northern Ireland features a severed, bloody limb known as the Red Hand of Ulster. Legend has it that well over a thousand years ago a marauding chieftain caught sight of the shores of Northern Ireland from the deck of his boat. He offered this green, fertile land to whichever of his two sons could first lay hand on it. Immediately his two sons began rowing furiously for the shore in their separate boats. One began to pull ahead, but the other, seeing his brother reaching the breakers, drew his sword, cut off his own hand, and threw it ahead of him onto the beach. Thus he was the first brother to lay hand on the new land.

violence is in fact restricted to certain areas in Northern Ireland and the Border district that are important politically, and many people enjoy a fun-loving, friendly, and peaceful life. However, for everyone in Ireland; especially those in Northern Ireland, the conflicts between the Catholic and Protestant communities cannot help but influence their lives. Wherever they go they may be searched for security reasons, and whenever they switch on the radio or television, they hear of bombs and terrorists' attacks. They may even have known the people who have been killed. Conversations come back to the "troubles" again and again as people voice their opinions on what they see as the solution.

Northern Ireland has become divided into two communities, Protestant and Catholic. They live in different areas, go to different schools, and meet at different places. This means that many Protestant and Catholic children never have the chance to meet one another. However, when they do get together in joint schools events or clubs, they are usually surprised to find they have much in common. Many people believe that if they can develop more understanding among young people, it would in time help to pave the way for peace. At present, however, this seems to be far in the future.

Outbreaks of violence

Northern Ireland first had its own parliament in 1920. For many years Northern Ireland was governed by the Unionists party which was supported by the majority of people. However, the Nationalist/Catholic minority objected to the fact that they had so little say in the country's government. They complained that the Protestants controlled all the councils (local governments and housing authorities) and gave the best houses and jobs to fellow Protestants.

These tensions grew and finally led to outbreaks of violence in the late 1960s. In 1969, riots broke out in Belfast and Londonderry (now called Derry, the city's original name). Houses and shops were set on fire and gasoline bombs were hurled at police. Many people were killed or injured. As a result of the rioting, the Prime Minister of Northern Ireland asked Britain for military help. British troops were brought in to help Northern Ireland's police force, the Royal Ulster Constabulary, and took up positions in known trouble spots.

Bloody Sunday

A few months later, the Irish Republican Army (IRA) split into the official IRA, who were non-violent, and the Provisional IRA, the "Provos," who began a full-scale terrorist attack on the British Army in Ireland. Civilians living in Northern Ireland became part-time soldiers and formed the Ulster Defense Regiment (UDR) to support the British Army.

Catholic feeling against the British was increased by the introduction of imprisonment without trial. This meant that people suspected of terrorist activities could be arrested and locked up without any means of defending themselves in court. The situation grew even worse on the day in January 1972 known as "Bloody Sunday,"

This impressive white stone building known as Stormont was once the headquarters of the parliament in Northern Ireland. It is about four miles east of Belfast in a lovely setting on top of a hill.

British troops were first sent to Northern Ireland in 1969 to help keep peace in certain trouble spots. They are still there to maintain law and order. Some soldiers patrol the streets to watch for any violence, others make security checks in stores and public buildings, some man the roadblocks on the borders between Northern Ireland and the Republic to watch for terrorists.

when a struggle between demonstrators and the British Army at a march in Derry led to the death of 13 Catholics.

At last matters became so bad that the British government suspended the parliament at Stormont and brought in a system of direct rule from London. This was only intended to be temporary, and in 1972, Britain and the Republic of Ireland formed an All-Ireland Council to try to arrive at an answer to the problem. They wanted to return to Northern Ireland some form of semi-independent parliament. Since then, several attempts to transfer government back to an elected Northern Ireland body (a process known as devolution) have been tried without success. Northern Ireland is therefore still ruled from

London, through the Secretary of State for Northern Ireland who is a minister in the British government.

Hunger strikes

Hostility between the two communities reached new heights toward the end of the 1970s, made even greater by the protest actions of IRA prisoners in the Maze Prison, Belfast. They felt that they should be treated as political prisoners and have more rights than criminal prisoners.

Several prisoners went on hunger strikes, and in May 1981, Bobby Sands died after 66 days without food or water. The hunger strikers were considered to be martyrs and their actions brought sympathy for the nationalist cause. A growing number of people in Northern Ireland began to join the Republican Sinn Féin party, which is the political arm of the IRA.

The Peace Movement

In August 1976, three young children were hit and killed by a car that was out of control. At its wheel was an IRA man who had been shot by a British soldier. These children were innocent victims. This tragic incident prompted their aunt, Mairead Corrigan, to join forces with Betty Williams and Ciaran McKeown to found the Peace People in Belfast. They wanted to encourage Catholics and Protestants to work together for peace. The Community of Peace People run peace centers, youth clubs, and job creation programs deliberately aimed at getting Catholics and Protestants to work together.

New Ireland Forum

The governments of Great Britain and the Republic of Ireland were both worried by this change in feeling. The two Prime Ministers met again in 1983 at the New Ireland Forum. They were joined by representatives of all the main political parties. The Forum came up with three possible answers to the problem: a united Ireland, a *confederal* Ireland in which both north and south would be part of one state but would each have its own parliament and keep its own identity, or the joint administration of Northern Ireland by the London and Dublin parliaments.

Anglo-Irish Accord

The idea of a united Ireland was the most popular with the Forum. This, however, was not acceptable to the Protestant majority in Northern Ireland and Britain had promised to respect the wishes of that majority. More violence followed. By the end of 1984, over 2,300 people had been killed and over 23,000 injured. A new agreement called the Anglo-Irish Accord was drawn up, giving the Irish government a say in the affairs of Northern Ireland. Although the Accord was welcomed by many, it also met with violent protest.

Most Irish nationalists would probably accept a confederal state or joint authority. Unionists, however, want Northern Ireland to be part of Great Britain or to have complete independence. Each solution put forward has met with opposition from one side or the other. The number of people dead is now nearing 3,000, and the end is still not in sight.

4 Agriculture

Agriculture brings in nearly a fifth of the national income. It is still the main way of life in rural Ireland, although industry is increasing. Even so, many people only farm part-time, working as part-time fishermen as well, for example. Most farms are either small or medium-sized, half of them being between 25 and 100 acres in size. However, there is a trend toward bigger farms.

Working the land

The way the land is used varies with its size and location in Ireland. The largest farms tend to be in the east of the country. There, each farm has an average of 64 to 81 acres of land, together with a

During the time of haymaking whole families can often be seen gathering the hay into stool-shaped stacks. However, this farmer has mechanized the work. Here the stacks are made by a machine that rolls them into a distinctive cylinder shape.

two-story farmhouse and numerous barns and outhouses. The east is the main crop-growing and livestock region. In contrast, farms in the west are small and often have only a single story, whitewashed farm cottage of the traditional style. In the most westerly part of County Cork and the western tips of County Mayo and County Galway, farm holdings are so small that these areas are known as the Western Small Farm Fringe. Farming there is very difficult because the land is poor and rocky, so it is used mainly for grazing cattle or sheep.

Almost all the agricultural land in Ireland is farmed by owners and their families who live on the land. In parts of the country farming is still carried out in the old-fashioned way, without modern machinery. Horses and donkeys are still used to pull plows, and at the end of the summer whole families can be seen in the fields making haystacks by hand. However, more machines are now being used, and it's easy to spot the difference between haystacks rolled by machine and the mushroom-shaped stacks made by hand.

Animals and crops

The mild climate in Ireland means that animals can be kept outdoors almost all year round. Factory farming (where large numbers of animals are kept indoors in confined, controlled conditions) is therefore practiced less in Ireland than anywhere else in Europe. Different animals are often kept together. However, poultry farming, which used to play a large part on farms in western Ireland, has changed. Small farmyard flocks have been replaced by large purpose-built poultry units in the east and the south. Although sheep and pigs are raised on farms, cattle are far more numerous. Ireland's rich grass is grazed by over two million cows which are kept either for beef or for milk production. The black and white Friesian cow is seen most often because it produces a great deal of milk and is also good for beef production. In hilly areas where the grass is poorer, sheep play a more important role.

Only one-tenth of Irish farmland is used to grow crops. In the east, where the soils are lighter and the climate is a little sunnier and drier, barley accounts for 50 percent of the crops grown. Some barley is grown for brewing beer and distilling whisky, but most of it is used as winter food for livestock. In the west, the wetter climate and more acid soils suit oat and potato crops, though some root crops are grown as animal fodder. Enough sugar beet is grown to supply the needs of the country. It is refined at factories in Carlow, Thurles, Mallow, and Tuam.

Selling at the local market

Some owners of small farms grow produce to be sold locally. Each week they take their potatoes, turnips, cabbages, or whatever is in season, to a nearby market and set up a stall. These farmers are careful to grow crops that ripen at different times of the year. In this way they avoid having too much to sell of any one particular vegetable. A typical local produce market is held every Saturday morning in Galway. A small side street is closed to traffic and farmers set up tables for their wares along the pavement. Some people

Towns and cities in Ireland all have market days. It's a popular day and a great chance for local people who may live in isolated places to meet friends and exchange news. All sorts of goods are offered, usually in small, very fresh batches.

with only a few goods to sell don't have a stall. Instead they stand on the street corner to sell their vegetables, perhaps from a bucket or a box. Still others use the trunks of their cars or the backs of their vans to display their goods. Foods sold at the market may include cheese, yogurt, honey, and fruit or meat pies, all often made from farm produce. The market is popular with shoppers because the produce is usually very fresh.

Since Ireland joined the European Economic Community (EEC) the farmer's life has started to change. Farms used to offer quite a poor standard of living. Income was low, and there was little money left over to develop the land. In addition, fewer people wanted to be farmers, and those who did were getting older. To some extent this trend has been altered by Ireland's sharing in the

A man and his donkey work the land with a small hand plow. Plows of this kind have been used by generations of farmers. Mechanized farming is usually in the north, but in the south where farms are smaller it is still developing.

The Common Agricultural Policy (CAP) is agreed on by members of the European Economic Community (EEC). CAP ensures a set price for goods produced by farmers in countries that belong to the Community. If the market price of an item falls below that agreed upon by CAP, the EEC will buy that produce and store it until demand is higher and a better price can be obtained. One major drawback to this system is that farmers may be encouraged to produce more than is needed which is a great waste of both money and food.

Common Agricultural Policy. This has brought money to allow farms to develop and earnings to increase. The market for Irish agricultural products has also widened to include the other member states in the EEC. Nevertheless, life on the farm remains hard work, even more so in regions where there has been little mechanization.

In Northern Ireland agriculture takes up 2.7 million acres, which is about 85 percent of the total land area. As in the Republic, rearing cattle for meat and dairy products is an important activity. However, there is more pig and poultry farming than in the Republic.

Agricultural shows are popular events, especially in the Republic. They are a chance to have a good time, to meet friends, and exchange news—have a "good crack," as the Irish say. There are all sorts of local events throughout the year, including sheep-shearing contests and horse-drawn plow matches. However, the really big events in the Republic are organized by the Royal Dublin Society. These include the Spring Show in May and the world famous Dublin Horse Show in August. In Northern Ireland the Royal Ulster Agricultural Society organizes a Spring Show in Belfast during May.

5   Trade and Industry

Technology is used in various workplaces in Ireland today. Here two people operate computer terminals in the office of the New York Life Insurance Company, in Castleisland, County Kerry.

In the past, Ireland has always been a farming country, with little trade or industry. However, today the picture is changing and Ireland has become more dependent on trading with other countries. The Republic's government, eager to increase industry, has provided financial help in recent years to companies willing to open factories and offices in country regions, since this brings work other than farming to rural areas. Although their policy has produced more widespread growth of manufacturing, the major industrial areas still remain in the east of Ireland and around Limerick in the west. Almost half of all Irish workers are found in the ports of County

Dublin, in Cork city and its harbor area, and in what is known as the Limerick-Shannon-Ennis triangle. Industrial firms tend to congregate near ports because it makes exporting goods easier, and also because they often depend on imported raw materials. The government has offered foreign companies help as well by reducing taxes and giving staff-training grants for workers in new industries. In the same way, in Northern Ireland the British government also offers tax relief grants toward buildings and machinery.

Manufacturing

Ireland's most important industry is manufacturing. It accounts for around 44 percent of the country's national income, 28 percent of its employment, and over 65 percent of all exports. The types of goods manufactured are varied. They include computers in Limerick, acid production (for use in food processing) in Cork, and glass in Waterford. One of Ireland's fastest growing manufacturing areas is that of metals and engineering. It also has a thriving pharmaceutical industry. Ireland ranks in the top 15 pharmaceutical exporting countries in the world. In addition, both clothing and textile industries export considerable quantities of goods. One of the biggest industries in Northern Ireland used to be shipbuilding. However, the demand for ships built in Northern Ireland has fallen and so the shipping companies have had to lay off many workers. This is one of the reasons why unemployment has increased in Northern Ireland which, like the Republic, has extensive unemployment problems.

Food and drink

The most well established Irish manufacturing industries are concerned with food and drink which produce more goods than other industry.

Soft drinks are manufactured in many towns and cities, but tend to be produced only for their own localities. Milling flour to provide bread is an important industry but this too is spread out all over Ireland.

Fishing

People who live surrounded by sea usually have a good fishing industry, but this is not the case with Ireland. The shallow seas have for centuries been fished by foreign fleets, but until fairly recently the Irish fleets faced many problems. As late as the 1960s the fishing boats were small and ill

What this photograph can't show is the smell! Killybegs is an important fishing town and the whole place smells very strongly of fish. Every day trawlers tie up here from many foreign ports. After they have been brought ashore the fish are taken for export or bought by restaurants throughout Ireland.

equipped and the harbors were poor. However, the main reason was the low demand for catches. Even today some Irish people think that only poor people eat fish.

The Irish Sea Fisheries Board (*Bord Iascaigh Mhara*) has in recent years tried to make changes. There are now over 2,500 full-time fishermen and 5,500 part-time fishermen working in the industry, with a further 1,500 people employed in fish-processing industries. However, this expansion has led to problems of supply. Over fishing of certain waters has brought a sharp decrease in fish numbers.

Fish are brought in at over 150 small harbors all around the coast, but the vast majority (about 50 percent) are brought ashore at Killybegs, Howth, Castletown Bere, Dunmore East, and Galway. Cod, whiting, haddock, herring, sprats, lobsters, oysters, crayfish, and prawns all form part of the catches. There are also fish farms, and commercial fishing on many estuaries and rivers. The main freshwater catch is salmon, but trout and eels are also frequently caught. In Northern Ireland, where all fishing takes place in the north Irish Sea, most of the catch is landed at the ports of Kilkeel, Ardglass, and Portavogie. Throughout Ireland, fishing for sport is enjoying a boom as part of the tourist industry.

Visitors to Ireland
The number of visitors to Ireland is growing each year and so the tourist trade is booming. The main attraction for people from overseas are the Irish way of life and the country's beautiful scenery. Despite developing industry, Ireland still has

To meet the ever-increasing demand from overseas tourists for handmade Irish gifts, small craft workshops are being opened. Throughout Ireland, but particularly in rural areas, traditional crafts skills are being revived. Here in Kilkenny Design Workshop a weaver is using a traditional loom.

large areas of unspoiled natural countryside and long stretches of deserted coastline. History is another important part of tourism and there are plenty of ruined castles, megalithic tombs, round towers, early Christian churches, and ancient settlements for visitors to see.

As tourism has grown, guest houses, hotels, shops, and restaurants have come into being along with it. Cottage industries have also flourished. Cottage industry is the name given to a very small-scale business, often run from a home or small workshop. In Ireland such industries include jewelry making, baked goods, and pottery. Tourism has produced a demand for souvenirs and in particular for items of traditional Irish crafts such as lace-making and weaving.

Two major centers for weaving are Donegal and Avoca. The weavers in both places produce distinctive colored fabric and high-quality garments, rugs, and accessories. For instance, the Avoca weavers use yarns dyed in the mauve, pink, and blue shades of local heather to weave cloaks, sweaters, scarves, and hats.

Hand weaving is done on a loom called a Fly Shuttle Loom. It was first used in 1740. At that time it caused riots, because it wove fabric very fast and the weavers were afraid of being put out of work. Since, today, most cloth is mass-produced at high speeds by mechanical means, the hand loom is used mostly to make very individual items.

The "troubles" and the image of violence on the streets, including apparently random bombings, have made many people decide not to spend their vacations in Northern Ireland, and the tourist industry is suffering. In order to help matters, the British government has provided grants so that the tourist trade can promote activities that are away from the trouble areas. Saltwater fishing and cruising along the coast are among the pursuits suggested for tourists.

Natural resources
One of the most important natural sources of fuel in Ireland is peat. Only the Soviet Union produces more peat than Ireland. In some parts of the country peat is still cut by hand as it has always been. However, mechanized cutting techniques have greatly speeded up the process

Peat has always been an important fuel in Ireland. It is sometimes cut by machines. However, the traditional hand-cutting method is more usual. When peat is harvested by hand, narrow sections of land are cut away and brick-shaped lumps of peat are left in large piles to dry out. Quite often the cut channels fill with water.

and now great areas of peat land are being scraped. Peat is used to generate electricity and there are seven peat-fired power stations in Ireland. Other important fuels are natural gas and oil, and Ireland is now exploring for these in Irish waters. Although coal is mined, it is only in fairly small amounts. Zinc ores are also mined, and one of the world's largest zinc and lead deposits is at Navan in County Meath. Other mining includes the quarrying of sand, gravel, and stone for the construction of industry and homes.

In Northern Ireland there is little mining apart from quarrying sand, grit, and gravel. However, some salt is produced near Carrickfergus. Imported fuel, mainly oil, is used to generate electricity and all the power stations are on the coast. The largest are Ballylukford and Kilroot which are both close to Belfast.

6 Communications

One of the many large ferry boats that travel between Great Britain and Ireland. Although the Irish Sea is only 120 miles wide at its widest point, it is often very rough and the journeys can take many hours.

Since Ireland is an island, transportation to Britain and to the European mainland is important. Both sea and air crossings are frequent all year round. The main commercial shipping ports are Belfast, Dublin, Cork, Limerick, Rosslare, Dun Laoghaire, Galway, Waterford, and Larne. The time it takes to cross from Ireland to Europe on a ferry depends on the route. It can, for example, take 4 hours to cross from Belfast to the Isle of Man, 2 hours to cross from Larne to Stranraer in Scotland, 8 hours to cross from Dublin to Liverpool in England, and 17 hours to cross from Wexford to Cherbourg in France. It is much quicker to fly. Ireland has three

Ireland's national airline celebrated its fiftieth anniversary in 1986. Here one of its jumbo jets is displayed beside one of the De Havilland Dragon biplanes used in 1936. The airline carries about two million passengers a year.

international airports at Dublin, Shannon, and Cork. In Northern Ireland the international airport is Belfast. Ireland's national airline, Aer Lingus, has flights traveling to 29 countries. The country is also served by nine other air transportation companies, the largest of which is Ryanair.

Traveling around

A huge 97 percent of travelers in Ireland, and about 84 percent of freight traffic, use its network of roads. The road system was developed during the nineteenth century to meet the needs of a much larger population than that of today. There are therefore a great many roads of all sizes, and

51

they are often empty. There is said to be 0.6 mile of road for every 34 people in Ireland. In cities like Dublin there can be traffic jams, especially during the morning and evening rush hours when most people travel to and from work. However, in rural areas traffic jams are only likely to occur if a farmer blocks the road with a herd of cows or stops a tractor in the middle of a lane to chat with a neighbor. The roads in Ireland vary in size from hard-surfaced highways to small single-lane dirt roads. There are superhighways in Northern Ireland, but only some 70 miles in its 14,700 mile road system. In Northern Ireland there are also roadblocks. These are check points set up across the road by the British Army. They can be anywhere, but are most often set up in and around the Border towns such as Newry and Derry. When stopped at a roadblock drivers must show some form of identification.

Like the road system, the railroad was also developed in Ireland during the nineteenth century. The railroads, now run by Córas Iompair Eireann, carry over 20 million passengers a year and about 650 million tons of goods such as mineral ores, cement, sugar beet, oil, and beer. Despite the commercial freight traffic, the 1,250-mile long railroad route operates at a loss. Northern Ireland presents a similar picture with only 210 miles of track. Part of the east coast of Ireland has a local electric train route known as the Dart, which connects coastal towns and resorts with Dublin. It is a popular form of transportation with commuters who live outside Dublin and have to travel into the city to work each day. The Dart is also used a great deal by

A modern Irish air-conditioned train, pulled by a diesel-electric locomotive, travels along a picturesque route passing a reconstructed early camp on the banks of a river.

families taking a day trip to the seashore, especially on weekends.

Buses are another way of traveling around Ireland. There are special school buses as well as local services, and long-distance buses that link major towns. In addition, there are also buses for tours and traveling across country. Bus tours operate mainly during the tourist season from April to September, and often take overseas visitors to some of Ireland's chief attractions such as the Cliffs of Moher.

53

Keeping in touch

There was a limited postal service between Dublin and London as early as 1561, but today the whole of Ireland is linked to the world by mail and by telecommunications. There are thousands of local post offices and even more of the distinctive green post boxes (bright red in Northern Ireland). Ireland is served by An Post (the Post Office) which employs over 11,000 people to handle over one million items of mail daily. In Northern Ireland, the postal service is the same as that in the United Kingdom and is known as the Royal Mail. One in five people have telephones in their own homes, but there are also telephones in public places and coin-operated telephones in major streets. Telecommunications in Ireland are managed by a state company called Bord Telecom Éireann. Its international services are provided through a network of radio links and submarine cable systems. It also has a transatlantic fiber-optic cable that allows many more telephone calls to go through. A satellite Earth station, at Midleton in County Cork, links Ireland with North America. There is a telex service to send messages and Bord Telecom Éireann can also transmit information over the telephone lines to a television screen when subscribers call for it.

News and views

Newspapers have been published in Ireland for just over 300 years. Ireland's first penny newspaper, which was read by a considerable number of people, was the *Irish Times*, first printed in 1859. Another historically important paper was the *Irish Press*, founded in 1931 by

Eamon De Valera, who later became President of Ireland. Nowadays, over five million copies of national papers are sold in Ireland every week. Six morning newspapers are published, of which three are based in Dublin: the *Irish Independent*, the *Irish Times*, and the *Irish Press*. One is published in Cork: the *Cork Examiner*. In Belfast there are two: *News Letter* and the *Irish News*. There are four evening newspapers: in Dublin the *Evening Press*, and the *Evening Herald*; in Belfast the *Belfast Telegraph*; and in Cork the *Evening Echo*. In addition, four Sunday newspapers are produced in Dublin and one in Belfast. There are also several provincial papers that are published weekly rather than daily and cover news of local interest. The best-selling local newspaper is the *Kerryman*. Numerous magazines and periodicals printed in Ireland can be found at newsstands beside magazines like *Vogue* from overseas.

Newspaper kiosks, like this one in the Dublin suburb of Ballsbridge, carry a range of magazines and newspapers from Great Britain and abroad as well as the Irish daily papers and some local papers such as the Kerryman.

Over the air waves

The national broadcasting organization in the Republic of Ireland is know as RTE which stands for Radio Telefis Éireann. It is a state-run company providing a whole range of television and radio broadcasting. Television programs include drama, features, news, education, sports, religion, and entertainment. These programs are broadcast through two channels, RTE 1 and RTE 2. Both channels can be received in most of Northern Ireland which also receives broadcasts from the BBC (British Broadcasting Corporation). Similarly, many homes in the Republic, particularly in the east, can watch BBC television programs. People often put up very high aerials on the roofs of their houses to pick up the transmissions.

Like television, radio in the Irish Republic has two channels, also called RTE 1 and RTE 2. Broadcasts are made both in English and in Irish, and the topics covered are much the same as those on television. In 1972 radio na Gaeltachta was established for the *Gaeltacht*, that is, for Irish-speaking listeners.

7   Education and Health

In the Republic of Ireland it is the law that all children between the ages of six and 16 must go to school. However, many children are sent to school when they are four and most attend by the time they are five. As there is no national system of nurseries or preschools in the Republic, these younger children attend the same first school as their older friends.

Many schools in Ireland are run by religious organizations. Here a nun is teaching a religious education class in Dublin's Roman Catholic Convent School.

In Northern Ireland, the British educational system is used and it is different from that of the Republic. It is administered locally by Education and Library Boards. Children must by law attend school between the ages of five and 16 and, like children in the south, they attend school on

weekdays. Unlike the Republic, nursery education is provided for children under five. All children are entitled to free schooling but there are a number of popular private schools that also attract pupils from overseas. There are two universities in Northern Ireland and two colleges of Education, as well as 26 Institutes of Further Education.

First school

The first schools children go to are called primary schools, or "national" schools. In the Republic of Ireland all primary education is free. It is paid for by the state, but the state does not provide or run the schools. A religious organization will ask the state for financial help to run a school. That school will then be managed by a group of people known as a Board of Management, which includes teachers, religious leaders, and parents. There are just under 3,400 primary schools in the Republic and around 575,000 children attend them. About 20,000 primary teachers are employed, which means that there are roughly 27 pupils to every teacher. Pupils stay at primary school for about eight years. All children also have to learn the Irish language, because the Republic of Ireland is eager to revive and promote this. There are now a number of schools where all subjects are taught in Irish. This applies especially in the Gaelic-speaking areas.

Most children go to primary school every weekday around 9:00 a.m. and stay until about 3:00 p.m. The day usually starts with a prayer followed by lessons. Boys and girls are taught together at first, but as they grow older are taught in separate classes. At the end of the day children are given homework that usually takes about an hour to do.

Children who are handicapped, such as blind or deaf children either have their own special schools to go to, or they attend separate classes attached to ordinary schools.

Getting older

After they leave primary school at the age of about 12, children attend secondary school. In the Republic there are four different types of secondary schools: vocational school, comprehensive school, community school, and voluntary secondary school. At one time vocational schools used to teach only manual skills and trades, but they now offer a full range of courses. There are 15 comprehensive schools in the Republic of Ireland. These are an experiment in combining academic subjects with more practical subjects. Community schools are similar to comprehensive schools, but are organized slightly differently. About two-thirds of all children in the Republic attend voluntary

In secondary schools in Ireland computers are now playing a large part in education. This class at St. Louise's Comprehensive in Falls Road, Belfast, is learning computer skills that may be used later in Ireland's expanding industries.

59

secondary school. Most of them go daily, but there are a few schools that take boarders.

Like primary schools, secondary schools are privately run, usually by religious groups. However, they do receive financial help from the state. About 90 percent of secondary schools offer free education, but quite often parents are expected to contribute as well.

Examinations

All schools enter their students for the same national examinations. Some pupils follow a two-year course leading to the Day Vocational Certificate which is known as the Group Certificate. There are 26 subjects on the curriculum, organized into five groups: Home Economics, Manual Training, Rural Science, and two groups of commercial subjects. Other students take a three-year course covering less-practical subjects that leads to the Intermediate Certificate. To gain the certificate pupils must take examinations in subjects that include Irish, English, history, geography, mathematics, science (or another language), commerce, civics, sports, and singing. By law students must have three years of secondary education, but after that they may leave school and about a quarter do so. Those who stay on at school follow a two-year course leading to a Leaving Certificate Examination. Some of these pupils continue at a university or an Institute for Higher Education.

Going to a university

There are two universities in the Republic of Ireland — the National University of Ireland

Founded in 1591, Trinity College is Ireland's oldest university. This is the cobbled courtyard at the center of the college. It's enjoyed by tourists and students alike who often walk through just to find somewhere peaceful to sit. The bell tower, or campanile, in the picture was built in 1853.

which was founded in 1908, and the University of Dublin, founded in 1591. The University of Dublin is just one college, called Trinity College, Dublin. The National University on the other hand has four colleges: Dublin, Cork, Galway, and Maynooth. Ireland also has two National Institutes for Higher Education, one in Dublin and one in Limerick. At these institutes students study mainly technology, applied science, and business administration, while at the universities students are more likely to study academic subjects such as literature and mathematics. However, all students are awarded the same level of qualification, called a degree.

More training

For young people who do not go on to further education after school, there are a number of training programs available. The Industrial Training Authority, for example, operates an apprentice training program in industry and commerce. Another organization called CERT trains people for work in tourism, hotel, and catering industries. It runs hotel and catering schools, and operates in-service training where young people work while they are learning a trade. A third organization, the Agricultural Training Authority, helps young people who want to work in agriculture.

Summer fun!
During the summer vacation large numbers of Irish children attend summer schools. These are held in country areas away from home, so that children can make friends with children from other parts of Ireland. Classes are held every day in subjects like art and sports, and they are taught in the Irish language. There are also classes in subjects of special interest to the Irish such as traditional music and dancing.

Health service

The health service of the nation is very important to the Irish government and people in the Republic are generally much healthier than ever before. This is because they have a better standard of living, better housing, and better food. Children today can expect to live longer than their grandparents. To help to keep Irish people well, the state provides a health and social security service that costs about one-third of the yearly budget. Employers and taxpayers make regular contributions to the service.

Keeping healthy

The health service is divided into six parts: community protection, community health services, community welfare, psychiatric services, services for the handicapped, and general hospital services. These services are for everyone to use, but they are not free except to people with a low income.

The range of health services offered includes visiting a general practitioner, known as a GP, who is a local doctor. A GP has an average of 920 patients. Local doctors see both public (that is, state-supported) and private patients. The hospitals are usually run by health boards, but sometimes by a religious organization. In addition, there are some hospitals that are privately run. For the care of eyes, ears, and teeth there are special services, which are once again both private and public.

It can be expensive to be sick, so many people insure themselves for medical costs. About one-third of the population of the Republic is insured with the Voluntary Health Insurance Board, the VHI.

Social welfare

Although the standard of living is improving throughout Ireland, there are still people who need help, such as those who are poor, have special needs, or are elderly.

Many hospitals in Ireland are run by religious orders. The statue of the Virgin Mary over the entrance to St. Vincent's Hospital, Dublin, shows that this is supported by the Catholic Church.

In the Republic, people who are unemployed, pregnant, or retired can receive social security payments to help them. Pensioners can travel free on local buses, but not every elderly person receives a pension. Elderly people are also entitled to some state support if they live in extended-care homes. However, there are not enough homes of this kind and they are often expensive. The state does not pay the entire cost.

In Northern Ireland

In Northern Ireland, the health service is free to everyone. This includes visiting the doctor and going to a hospital. However, some people prefer to visit a hospital or see a doctor as private patients. One reason for this is that there are often long waiting lists for hospital treatment. Although there are criticisms of the health service, it does offer a good standard of treatment for everyone. Retirement pensions, unemployment benefits, and aid to children are all paid by the Department of Health and Social Services.

8 People and Their Families

Many people are surprised that the center of Belfast is such a bright place. Despite the "troubles" it is a very busy city with many people working in offices and shopping in the stores. In recent years, old buildings have been renovated, new ones have been built, and more facilities for recreation have been opened.

Ireland is one of the least populated countries in Europe. There are around five million people living there altogether. One-third of the people live in Northern Ireland and the other two-thirds in the Republic of Ireland. Northern Ireland is much smaller than the Republic and is more densely populated.

The majority of people live in towns and cities where there are now many new public housing projects. These have been built to accommodate families who have moved in from the country to find work. Belfast is the capital city of Northern

Ireland and a surprisingly large number of the country's population lives here. It is said that about a third of the population of Northern Ireland lives and works within ten miles of Belfast's city hall.

The population of the Irish Republic is mainly concentrated in the east and south, with fewer people living in the more rural west. Nearly one million people live in the capital city of Dublin. It is not a big city compared with other capitals such as Paris with nearly nine million, or London with nearly seven million people. However, Dublin is home to about a quarter of the total population of the Republic.

Until recent years most people lived in the rural areas of Ireland, but because of the high rate of unemployment many families have now moved to live in the main cities and towns where there is more chance of finding a job. Homes in urban areas are mainly attached houses built in rows along streets. There are also many new housing developments in the suburban areas of the cities. Houses are usually two stories high and designed to accommodate single families. In some rural areas housing has become very overcrowded and people are living in bad conditions. In country areas people often live in single-story cottages, most of which are many years old. A traditional Irish cottage was built from whatever materials and local stone could be found nearby. The walls are whitewashed and the roof is thatched. Around three-quarters of homes in Ireland are owned by the families who live in them. Houses and apartments are also provided by local authorities for people living in poor

Travelers move from place to place to make a living. They live in trailers and the children have difficulty getting an education since they change schools so often.

accommodations or families with special needs such as the elderly or handicapped.

A group of around 3,000 families in Ireland are known as Travelers. They do not live in houses at all but move from place to place, trying to make a living from dealing in scrap metal or trading horses.

Family life

Until recently families in Ireland were large, often with as many as ten children, but nowadays people do not have so many children. Family ties are very strong in Ireland. People usually live near their relatives and know they can rely on one another for help when needed. It is so difficult to find jobs, however, that many young people do not have much hope for the future. Some decide to emigrate to start a new life in another country, but steps are being taken to try to give them more reason to stay.

Ireland has a long history of emigration. After the Great Famine of 1845 hundreds of thousands of people left to set up homes in other countries, especially America, Great Britain, Australia, New Zealand, and South America. Descendants of those families are now becoming interested in tracing their roots, and many visit Ireland to find their relatives. Such prominent Americans as Presidents John F. Kennedy and Ronald Reagan, automobile magnate Henry Ford, and the tennis player John McEnroe have Irish ancestors.

The Blarney Stone
Irish people have a reputation for lively, witty conversation and also powerful and influential speeches. The word "Blarney" is sometimes used to describe the way they talk. Stories about how this name came to be used all center on the Blarney Stone. According to one legend, it was a present from a witch who had been saved from drowning. She promised that anyone who kissed the stone would be granted the gift of eloquence, that is, persuasive speech. True or not, Blarney Castle in County Cork attracts thousands of tourists who come to kiss the Blarney Stone.

Two languages
The Republic of Ireland has two official languages, English and Irish. Road signs, for example, are usually in both English and Irish. Irish is a Gaelic language. Until the eighteenth

Although most people in Ireland speak English, the official language in the Republic is Irish. All over Ireland there are many shop signs and road signs written in both languages. Many of the signs help to direct tourists to hotels and places such as the Black Valley Youth Hostel.

century many people still used Irish in everyday life, but by the beginning of this century it was spoken by very few people. The government feared that the Irish language might die out so in recent years it has been made a compulsory subject in most schools. Children are encouraged to read Irish books and to write stories in Irish. There are radio and television program in Irish and also some newspapers.

The Gaeltacht
Irish is still spoken regularly in certain districts known as the Gaeltacht. In these areas all the shop signs and road signs are in Irish, and people

listen to an all-Irish radio station. About 10,000 people speak Irish as a first language. Children and adults can go to Gaeltacht colleges to learn more about the language, and there is a Gaeltacht theater and also an airline. Some people wear traditional dress and old crafts are still practiced.

Ancient customs still survive in the Gaeltacht and other country areas of Ireland. A St. Brigid's cross woven from rushes or straw may be seen hanging above the front doors of houses or in barns. These crosses were once believed to protect families and livestock from evil. Some old customs mark important dates in the agricultural year. May Day, for example, celebrates the beginning of the farming year, and Halloween marks the end. Potatoes still in the ground at Halloween will be left there, and children are not to pick blackberries after that date.

Going to Church
People in Ireland are free to follow any religion they choose, and the Irish are known as a deeply religious nation. The Roman Catholic faith is particularly strong in the Republic. About 93 percent of the people there are Catholics and most of them attend Mass regularly. Around two-thirds of the people in Northern Ireland are Protestant, and belong to either the Church of Ireland, the Presbyterian Church, or the Methodist Church. There are also some Irish people of the Jewish faith.

The powerful influence of religion reaches into all walks of life in both the Republic and Northern Ireland. As it has been noted in previous chapters for the majority of people their religion,

St. Patrick

On March 17 each year Irish people all over the world celebrate with parades, singing, and dancing. It is the feast day of St. Patrick, the patron saint of Ireland. St. Patrick was born in Britain in the year 385, and when he was 16 he was captured by pirates in a slave raid. He was brought over to Ireland where he worked for six years as a slave, taking care of sheep and cattle, before he managed to escape. He returned years later as a bishop and began to travel around the country converting people to Christianity. A tradition on St. Patrick's Day is to wear a sprig of shamrock, because according to legend, St. Patrick used the three-leaved shamrock to explain the Holy Trinity.

Many places in Ireland have strong associations with St. Patrick. One is Downpatrick in County Down where a stone slab inscribed "PATRIC" marks the spot where he is said to be buried. Another is Croagh Patrick, Ireland's holy mountain, in County Mayo. St. Patrick fasted for 40 days and nights on the top of the mountain and each year pilgrims retrace his steps, often in bare feet, to the summit for a Mass.

Protestant or Catholic, often determines the schools they go to, the sports and social clubs they join, and the political parties they support. In some areas, people usually only marry someone of the same religion.

The Catholic Church maintains strict moral codes that Catholics are expected to follow. From a very young age children learn the teachings of the Catholic faith. They say their prayers at morning, night, and before their meals, and they

Most people in Ireland go to church. In Northern Ireland, the majority go to Protestant churches but in the Republic a very high percentage are Roman Catholics. There are many very beautiful churches, even in small villages on the Aran Islands.

read stories about the courage and virtue of the famous saints as an example of how they should lead their lives. At children's First Communions, which are usually around their seventh birthday, they are welcomed into the Catholic Church. It is a very special day. All the family is there. On this day the children can choose the name of a saint to add to their own names.

In many parts of Ireland saints are associated with towns and villages. These local saints each have a special day devoted to them. People of the area gather together to pray at little "stations" by the roadside. There are sometimes fairs and colorful parades, too. All over Ireland important dates in the Christian calendar such as Easter and Christmas are celebrated in churches and homes with special prayers, hymns, and processions.

9 Sports and Leisure

In Ireland most people enjoy playing or watching sports in their spare time. All forms of sports involving horses are popular, because the Irish are especially fond of horses. Race horses bred in Ireland have a high reputation for their speed and power, and races attract large crowds. One of the most famous racetracks in Ireland is The Curragh in County Kildare, where the Irish Derby and other important races are run. The horse races known as "steeplechases" have their origins in Ireland. Back in 1752, two men from Cork raced each other on horseback from Buttevant Church to the spire of St. Leger Church over a 4.5 mile course with open fields, hedges, walls, and

Horse shows and sports are very popular all over Ireland. These horses are taking part in a trotting race. It is an ancient sport dating back to Roman days. Some trotting races are held in a big arena, others are in village streets and fields. People usually place a bet and there is always a lot of noise and cheering.

ditches. This contest was the beginning of a new sport, "steeplechasing," where horse and rider must jump fences in the course of a race. Show jumping competitions are held regularly in every part of Ireland. The most important is the Dublin Horse Show which has entrants from all over the world.

With so much open space and pleasant countryside, trail-riding has become popular and over the past few years many trail-riding centers have opened. They organize vacations for people of all ages.

Sports for all

Many people are enthusiastic anglers and fish either in the sea or in the lakes and rivers. Golf is also a favorite and there are more than 250 golf courses, including several championship courses. Ireland is ideal for water sports with 3,500 miles of coastline and many lakes and rivers. Sailing has been popular for a long time and the world's oldest sailing club is the Royal Cork Yacht Club, founded in 1720. In recent years people have found the waters right for wind-surfing, surfing, canoeing, and scuba diving.

Inspired by the success of Irish racing cyclists Sean Kelly and Stephen Roche, many would-be champions have now decided to test their skills at cycling. Athletics, especially running, is also becoming very popular and marathon races are held annually in Belfast, Dublin, Cork, and other towns and cities. Other sports enjoyed in Ireland are soccer, which is played at all levels from schoolboy to senior citizen, rugby, tennis, swimming, and hockey.

Hurling is one of Ireland's national sports. It is a very spectacular sport to watch. The game is played in schools, villages, and towns. The best hurling players are on the county teams like these players. Big crowds come to watch county games but even small games have plenty of supporters.

Gaelic games

The traditional Gaelic games of hurling and Gaelic football are played throughout the Republic and in some parts of Northern Ireland. Children learn these national games at school and often continue to play for local teams when they leave school. Hurling has been played in Ireland since prehistoric times and is one of the fastest ball-and-stick games in the world. Girls play a version called *camoige*. This is a team game with 15 people on each side, and is played with sticks known as hurleys and a small, leather-covered ball. The rules are quite simple but the game is so fast and skillful that spectators often find it difficult to follow the action. Gaelic football is a field game similar to soccer except that the players are allowed to pick up the ball and run with it.

Both hurling and Gaelic football are played by amateurs and there are no paid professional players as in other sports. Gaelic sports competitions are held at least once a week between teams from different towns and villages. Many families go to watch their local team playing in a Sunday afternoon game. Each year teams from the 32 counties of Ireland (that is, both from the Republic and from Northern Ireland) compete for a place in the All-Ireland hurling and Gaelic football finals. These are held at Croke Park in Dublin, the largest sports stadium in Ireland. The finals are so popular with spectators that it is difficult to get a ticket, but followers can watch at home because the games are televised.

Road bowls or "bullets," a most extraordinary and sometimes dangerous game, is another national sport but it is now only played in the counties of Armagh and Cork. Two players throw a heavy, metal ball along a course on a winding public road, and the winner is the one who can cover the distance in the fewest throws. At one time, this game was illegal but very few people get into trouble for playing it now. Road bowls is a betting sport and large amounts of money are wagered at contests.

The great outdoors
The countryside has so much variety that it's no surprise to find that walking and mountaineering are favorite pastimes. There are several scenic, long-distance footpaths such as The Ulster Way

Both tourists and Irish families from the cities enjoy being in the countryside. As roads are so quiet, one very popular way of touring is by the traditional horse-drawn covered wagon.

and The Wicklow Way, and many mountain and moorland trails. Often people combine walking with bird-watching. A great deal of importance is placed on conservation of wildlife and a considerable number of nature sanctuaries have been set up. Forest and country parks are favorite places for families to visit on weekends. These beautiful parks often have cafes, shops, picnic areas, sign-posted walks, nature trails, and other amenities. Some also provide camping and trailer sites. Over recent years more historic houses and gardens have been opened to the public. Several are still lived in by the descendants of the families who built them.

There are not many organized activities for children in Ireland, especially in the more remote areas. Young people make their own fun by playing games in the streets or exploring the countryside.

At the fair
Fair day was once very important for people in Ireland. Fairs and festivals are now making a comeback, with many traditional and modern

---

Public Holidays

Northern Ireland
New Year's Day (January 1)
St. Patrick's Day (March 17)
Good Friday
Easter Monday
May Day holiday
Spring Bank holiday
Orangeman's Day (July 12)
Summer Bank holiday
Christmas Day
Boxing Day (December 26)

Republic of Ireland
New Year's Day (January 1)
St. Patrick's Day (March 17)
Good Friday
Easter Monday
June holiday (First Monday)
August holiday (First Monday)
October holiday (Last Monday)
Christmas Day
St. Stephen's Day (December 26)

This wild goat is the centerpiece of the ancient Puck Fair, a horse and cattle fair, which is held at Killorgan for three days in August every year. The goat, or ''Puck'' as he is known, is brought down from the mountains. No one is quite sure of the origin of this custom but many think it is a sort of ancient pagan fertility rite.

festivals of music, dance, sports, and food being held in towns and villages. One of Ireland's oldest and biggest fairs is the Oul' Lammas Fair in Ballycastle. An old Irish song says, "You can take your Mary Ann for some dulse and yellow man at the Oul' Lammas Fair at Ballycastle O!" and these two local delicacies are still sold at the fair. "Dulse" is dried seaweed and "yellow man" is a slab of sweet brittle toffee. The Puck fair in Killorgan, County Kerry, has also been held for several hundred years. A goat known as "King Puck" is decorated with ribbons, and watches over the three days of festivities from a raised platform. The Rose of Tralee International Festival, which is a beauty contest, now attracts visitors from all over the world. A carnival is held, with fireworks, music, and street dancing as well as the Tralee horse races.

79

Traditional Fare

Irish people have a long tradition of good breadmaking. Their specialty is white and brown soda bread which is nutty, crumbly, and very tasty. Another type of bread known as Barm Brack is always eaten at Halloween (October 31). Barm Brack is spicy and fruity. When it is being prepared, a ring is included in the mixture, and it is said that whoever gets the ring will be married within a year. Other dishes associated with Ireland are Irish Stew made with mutton, onions, and potatoes; spiced beef which is eaten at Christmas; potato cakes and potato scones, and Dublin Coddle, a Saturday night supper dish with bacon, sausages, onions, and potatoes.

Irish hospitality

Most homes have a television and there are a variety of programs to watch during the day and evening. People living in towns and cities also enjoy going to the theater and movies. In country areas, social life particularly for men tends to revolve around the pub. There are plenty of pubs and hotel bars where adults can meet for a chat and often a sing-song or traditional music session. Guinness is Ireland's most famous drink for adults. Next comes whisky which has been drunk in Ireland for more than 500 years. In Ireland the word *whiskey* is spelled with an *e* and comes from the Irish *uisce beatha* which means water of life. Irish coffee is made with whisky and sweetened black coffee topped with cream.

Eating out in a restaurant in Ireland can be rather expensive especially in the Republic, so

Irish soda bread is one of the specialities of the country. The traditional recipe is still used in many homes. It is very easy to make but many people buy it at the bakery. The ingredients are flour, buttermilk, baking soda, and salt. It is delicious alone or eaten with cheese.

although some families enjoy Sunday lunch in a hotel most people have their meals at home. Traditional Irish cooking is very simple but plates are usually piled high with food. A typical meal in an Irish home might be bacon and cabbage casserole; bacon, eggs, and potato cakes, or ham and French fries with several different types of bread. Irish people enjoy company and are usually very hospitable.

81

10 The Arts

Centuries ago, every small community in Ireland had its own storyteller. These men and women used to entertain people for hours with tales of heroes and warrior-kings. Monks later wrote down many of the ancient myths and legends in the old Gaelic language, decorating the initial letters and adding sketches. Such manuscripts are called "illuminated" manuscripts. *The Book of the Dun Cow* dates back to the twelfth century and others to even earlier times. These old books are full of epic sagas of tragedy, love, brave deeds, and great battles. The legends have inspired many Irish writers and artists.

One artist who used Irish legends as a theme for some of his paintings was Jack B. Yeats, brother of the poet, William B. Yeats. Many of his paintings and those of other well-know Irish artists such as James Latham, Francis Danby, and Paul Henry are hanging in the National Gallery of Ireland in Dublin. When the National Gallery opened in 1864 it had only 188 paintings on display. Today it has a good collection of over 2,500 oil paintings, almost 3,500 drawings and watercolors, and nearly 250 pieces of sculpture. There are galleries in towns and cities throughout Ireland and exhibitions are held regularly, often featuring the work of contemporary artists.

A way with words
Many well-known authors, poets and play-wrights were born and lived in Ireland. Writers have often had strong links with specific parts of

This is the National Gallery of Ireland, in Dublin. Many fine works of art from different periods are exhibited, including paintings by such master artists as Michelangelo, Rubens, Goya, and Gainsborough. There are several Irish Rooms. These hold works by Irish artists and portraits of Irish personalities over three centuries.

the country. James Joyce, for example, was born in Dublin in 1882 and spent the first 22 years of his life there. During that time he lived at 18 addresses so that he eventually knew every street and square. His most famous work, *Ulysses*, describes in minute detail a day in the life of a Dubliner named Leopold Bloom. Great Irish writers include Jonathan Swift who wrote *Gulliver's Travels*, Oliver Goldsmith, author of the play *She Stoops to Conquer*, Oscar Wilde, George Bernard Shaw, William Butler Yeats, John Synge, Sean O'Casey, and Samuel Beckett.

(Left) The Irish have a long history, most of which has been passed down by songs and poems. This bronze statue in Grafton Street, Dublin, is one of their most famous characters, Molly Malone, a young fish peddler who died tragically.

William Butler Yeats (1865–1939)
The area around Sligo is known as "Yeats country." This was where the great poet spent his boyhood years and where he is buried, in Drumcliffe churchyard five miles north of Sligo town. Yeats writes of the beauty of the countryside in his poems. He was also fascinated by the legendary past of Ireland, often using it as a theme. Two of his most celebrated works are *The Tower* and *The Winding Stair*. Yeats played an important part in the revival of theater in Ireland. He was one of the founders of the Abbey Theatre in Dublin which opened in 1904 with three one act plays by Yeats. He was awarded the Nobel Prize for literature in 1923.

W. B. Yeats was one of many famous writers Ireland has produced. His connections with the Abbey Theatre in Dublin helped to make it one of Ireland's leading theaters.

85

For a country of its size, Ireland has a surprising number of theaters, and performances, whether professional or amateur, are well attended. One of the best known theaters is the Abbey Theatre in Dublin, opened in 1904. The Abbey quickly gained an international reputation, and was especially noted for performances of plays by Irish playwrights on Irish subjects. Irish playwrights have always presented their latest work there, including George Bernard Shaw and Sean O'Casey. One play, *Playboy of the Western World* by John Synge, was so controversial when it was first produced in 1907 that it led to riots in the theater.

Ireland also has a National Folk Theatre known as *Siamsa Tire*. The show is a mixture of dance, song, and Irish folklore. Dressed in colorful native costume, the performers use song and

---

George Bernard Shaw (1856–1950)
Shaw was born in Dublin. Although his family was well born, they were poor, and his father drank a great deal. "Ginger," as Shaw was known, was a lonely young man, spending many hours at the National Gallery in Dublin. Indeed, he was so grateful to the Gallery for everything it taught him that he left a large sum of money to it when he died. A statue of Shaw stands by the entrance. In his long life he wrote many works that are internationally renowned. Among his most famous plays are *Saint Joan, Caesar and Cleopatra*, and *Pygmalion*. In recognition of his talent, Shaw was awarded the Nobel Prize for literature in 1925.

Some Key Twentieth-century Irish Writers

George Moore (1852-1933) novelist. His collection *The Untilled Field* (1903) inspired the short-story movement in Ireland.

Liam O'Flaherty (1897-1984), nationalist and novelist, chiefly known for his short stories. His novel *The Informer* (1925) was filmed by the Irish-American director, John Ford, in 1935.

Sean O'Faolain (b. 1900) Gaelic scholar, influenced by Chekhov as in *A Nest of Gentlefolk* (1937).

Flann O'Brien (Brian O'Nolan) (1911-1966) was influenced by James Joyce, and wrote satirical comedies like *At-swim-two-birds* (1930).

Julia O'Faolain, daughter of Sean O'Faolain, novelist and short-story writer whose dark comedy is often concerned with the position of women in society.

Edna O'Brien (b. 1932) Short-story writer, playwright and novelist who first came to fame with *The Country Girls* in 1960.

Maeve Binchy, novelist and short-story writer whose reputation was established in the 1980s with works like *London Transports* and *The Lilac Bus.*

Christy Nolan (b. 1966) whose collection of poetry, *Dam-burst of Dreams* (1981), and autobiographical work *Under the Eye of the Clock* (1987) brought this severely handicapped, but original young poet to prominence in the 1980s.

mime to recreate scenes from bygone days on the farm. There's a tune for each farmyard activity: a thatching song, a song for feeding the chickens , a song for milking the cows, and a song for making butter.

Making music

Music has always been important to the Irish. They enjoy singing and playing music with family and friends at home, and in any village there will be music coming from at least one or two houses in the evening. Hundreds of years ago, the official poet and musician was the bard, who was greatly respected and held a high place in society. In medieval times, wandering minstrels used to travel around the country, singing songs and ballads, and accompanying themselves on a harp. They were always made welcome by kings and chieftains who gave them food, drink, and a bed in return for entertainment. The tunes were not written down until around 1792, when a man named Edward Bunting put together a collection for the Great Harp Festival in Belfast. Since then collectors and performers have been writing down tunes, and in recent years traditional Irish music has become popular in Ireland and overseas.

Song and dance

There are many Irish folk musicians playing in Ireland today. One well-known group is The Chieftains, who have made several records and have toured in many different countries, including the United States. The highlight of the traditional music year is the All-Ireland Fleadh

These musicians are entertaining an audience in a bar in County Donegal. In recent years, traditional music has become very popular with visitors. Irish people love to sing and many pubs and hotels now hold music nights featuring Irish ballads. Customers are expected to join in, too.

(pronounced "Flah"). This is a three day festival of music and song with competitions for musicians from all over the world. There are also smaller music festivals held in towns and villages throughout the year. Pubs and hotels often hold regular traditional music nights which are always popular with local people and visitors.

The harp is an instrument associated with Irish music. However, these days it is rarely played except in concert halls or at medieval banquets held in old castles as a tourist attraction. The sounds of the fiddle, accordion, tin whistle, Irish bagpipes, and perhaps the *bodhran* are more likely to be heard at a music session today. A *bodhran* is a small drum something like a tambourine, and is made by stretching a piece of goatskin over a round frame. It is played with the knuckles or a double-ended drumstick.

The art of folk dancing is also still very much

part of life in Ireland. It is bright and lively with energetic foot-stamping and hand-clapping. The steps of Irish folk dancing used to be taught by dancing masters who traveled around the country, staying at farmhouses and giving lessons night after night until their pupils got it exactly right. Children are still taught the steps and love to dance. Parties called *ceilidhs* (pronounced kay-lees) are held in homes, halls, and outdoors so that people of all ages can get together to dance Irish reels and jigs and sing the old songs. They are usually happy occasions and visitors are made very welcome.

Traditional Irish music and dance has a large following, but Irish people like to listen and often dance to other types of music, too. There are many different bands and individual musicians playing pop music, country, jazz, gospel, classical, and other music, and concerts are held throughout Ireland. Many Irish musicians and rock groups such as Van Morrison and U2 have become internationally famous. One pop singer, Bob Geldof, who was the lead singer with the Dublin-based group, The Boomtown Rats, became famous throughout the world for raising huge sums of money to help starving people in Ethiopia. He organized the Live Aid rock concert, involving many well-known groups and singers, that was held partly in Philadelphia and partly in London. It was televised the world over.

On film
Another major art form enjoyed in Ireland is the movies. Although many movie theaters in country areas have now closed down they are still

The Irish rock group U2 performs all over the world. A film called Rattle and Hum *was released in 1988. It was of their tour of the United States.*

to be found in cities and towns. There are currently about 120 theaters. Irish film has had a big revival in recent years. The country has been chosen as a location for several films including *Educating Rita*, which was filmed at Trinity College, Dublin. The much acclaimed *Ryan's Daughter* was made by an Irish crew and filmed on the wild and rugged Dingle Peninsula. Remains of the buildings made for the film can still be seen. In recent years films for both movies and television have been made to show what life is like in Ireland today. One of these , *Cal*, is about the "troubles" in Northern Ireland. It was praised by both the critics and the public.

The future
Ireland is a country that has always been the home of many people with energy and talent. Some of these people have been forced to leave this beautiful island in times of trouble, but they have taken their natural enthusiasm to establish a life in young countries such as the United States, Canada, or Australia. These countries have strong ties with Ireland and although they are often distressed to see the fighting and violence they can also see that Ireland is still a thriving country.

Index

Lady's Day 30
Land Acts 25
language 68, 69, 70
Larne 50
Latham, James 82
Leinster 17, 20
Liffey River 18
Limerick 13, 43, 44, 50

Mallow 39
Maze Prison 35
monarchs 16
  Brian Boru 19
  Earl of Pembroke,
    "Strongbow" 20
  Elizabeth I, of England 20
  Henry II, of England 20
  James II, of England 21
  William of Orange 5, 21
mountains 7, 11, 12
  Connemara 11–12
  Mourne 11
Munster 17

National Folk Theatre (*Siamsa
  Tire*) 86
National Gallery of Ireland 82
national parks
  Connemara 11, 12
  North Antrim Coast 11
National University of Ireland 61
Nationalists 29, 30, 32, 35, 36
natural resources 7, 8, 48, 49
  coal 49
  gas and oil 49

minerals 49
  peat 7, 8, 48, 49
Neolithic period 15, 16
Newgrange 15, 16
New Ireland Forum 36
New Model Army 21
Newry 14, 52

O'Casey, Sean 83, 86
O'Connell, Daniel 23
Orangemen 29, 30

Parnell, Charles Stewart 25
partition 12, 27, 29, 30
Peace Movement 35
Pearse, Patrick 26
peat 7–8, 48, 49
planters 5, 20, 21
plant-life 10, 11
population 14, 24, 65, 66
Portavogie 46
Puck Fair 79

Radio Telefís Éireann (RTE) 56
railroads 52, 53
religion 22, 23, 30, 31, 58, 70
  Catholic 21, 22, 23, 30, 31, 32,
    70–72
  Protestant 20, 22, 30, 31, 32,
    70, 71
republicanism 22, 23, 24, 25, 26,
  27, 28, 33, 36
rivers 7, 18
road bowls 76
road travel 51, 52